UNITED STATES CRYPTOLOGIC HISTORY

Series V
The Early Postwar Period, 1945-1952
Volume 5

The Invisible Cryptologists:

African-Americans,

WWII to 1956

by

Jeannette Williams

with

Yolande Dickerson, Researcher

CENTER FOR CRYPTOLOGIC HISTORY
NATIONAL SECURITY AGENCY
2001

Table of Contents

The origins of this book were in the cryptologic equivalent of an urban legend and a couple of photographs.

During research on the early days of NSA, historians at the Center for Cryptologic History (CCH) learned of the employment of African-Americans at the Agency in the period after World War II. Occasionally, in informal conversations with former NSA seniors, the subject of minority history would come up, and CCH historians collected anecdotes about segregated offices in the early days. It became apparent that the employment of African-Americans came even earlier than previously thought. No information, however, confirmed any contribution by African-Americans during the world war.

In early 1996, the History Center received as a donation a book of rather monotonous photographs of civilian employees at one of NSA's predecessors receiving citations for important contributions. Out of several hundred photographs, only two included African-Americans – an employee receiving an award from Colonel Preston Corderman (reproduced on page 14) and the same employee posing with his family.

Although undated, the matrix of the photograph indicated it had been taken in 1945 or early 1946. This made it likely the person was receiving an award for wartime contributions.

It therefore became a high priority in the History Center to investigate the story behind this photograph and learn the truth behind the unconnected anecdotes about African-Americans in the early days of the cryptologic organization.

In 1998 it became possible to hire a few additional historians for a year to supplement the History Center's permanent staff. Ms. Jeannette Williams applied to research the early history of African-Americans in cryptology.

Assisted by Ms. Yolande Dickerson, Ms. Williams undertook an exhaustive search of the cryptologic archives and recovered the basic story of the segregated cryptologic organizations – including the previously unknown existence of a large office of African-Americans in World War II.

The basic facts about this unit preserved in official records, however, shed little light on the social milieu of the time or the eventual movement of African-Americans into the cryptologic mainstream.

Compiling – and constantly expanding – a list of names of African-Americans who worked in the early days of NSA and its predecessor organizations, they conducted an exceedingly vigorous program of oral history interviews. These interviews personalized the stark facts found in the documents.

In fact, this monograph rescues an important historical story that might otherwise have been lost. It should also be noted that this was a last-minute rescue. Several important figures had already passed away by the time the research for this book began, and several more have passed away between the time of their interviews and the publication of this book.

The story that the author tells is by turns infuriating and inspiring. But it needs to be faced squarely from both these aspects.

I recommend *The Invisible Cryptologists: African-Americans, WWII to 1956* as essential reading for all who are interested in the early days of cryptology, all who are interested in the social history of NSA and its predecessors, and all who are interested in the history of American race relations.

For further background on cryptologic activities during World War II and the early days of NSA, readers are encouraged to refer to *A History of U.S. Communications Intelligence during World War II: Policy and Administration* by Robert L. Benson and *The Origins of the National Security Agency* by Thomas L. Burns (forthcoming). Both publications are available from the Center for Cryptologic History.

David A. Hatch
Director, Center for Cryptologic History

Acknowledgments

My friend and assistant, Yolande Dickerson, must share the credit for whatever is right with this book. Appointment setter, record keeper, transcriber, and researcher – she did it all, and with marvelous good cheer. Thank you, Yolande.

For the inspiration that sparked this project and for critical reviews of many drafts, I am thankful to Dr. David Hatch of the Center for Cryptologic History (CCH). Dr. Thomas Johnson, formerly of the Center, was my early mentor, and I am indebted to him for his professional guidance and quick friendship. Others at NSA that must be remembered at this time are the Archives Division staff, particularly Danny Wilson, Mike Scott, John Hanson, and Tom Lubey, who were so responsive to my many, many requests; Barry Carleen and Barbara Vendemia of the CCH Publications team, for their skillful editing; Lou Benson and Patricia Brown, Office of Security, for historical information on security matters; and Patricia Nelson of the Phoenix Society, for providing critical data that enabled us to contact numerous Agency retirees.

James Gilbert, INSCOM Historian, deserves special recognition for directing me to an Army history that named the early African-American cryptologists. John Taylor of the National Archives and Records Administration also provided important lead information as well as outstanding file retrieval support. Thank you, John.

For the support of my husband Walter, daughter Darice, son Erik, and sister Thomasina, I am and always will be deeply grateful. They understood that, given the opportunity, I was obligated to write this history, not only to document the contributions of the early African-American cryptologists to the Agency's mission, but also to help identify for today's cryptologists the roots of the racial concerns that plagued NSA for decades afterwards. If I have, in any small way, met this obligation, it is due to the unselfish participation of the many former Agency employees who told me their stories. To them, my profoundest thanks. To the African-Americans among them who served at Arlington Hall, I am particularly grateful, for though the memories were sometimes painful, they freely shared their experiences, their disappointments, and their successes. To them, this book is fondly dedicated.

Jeannette Williams

This is the story of African-Americans employed by the National Security Agency, and its forerunners at Arlington Hall Station, from 1939 to 1956. It is, in part, an organizational history, since for most of that period, the overwhelming majority of African-Americans were segregated in primarily support elements, consistent with army policies and U.S. mores. It is also, in part, a cryptologic history, since technology and intelligence requirements factored enormously into African-American hiring and manpower utilization. For these aspects of the book, documents held in the NSA Archives as well as in the National Archives and Records Administration yielded a wealth of information.

But at its essence this book is about people who during WWII and the first decade of the Cold War were limited primarily to positions in the federal agency akin to those held in the private sector – critical, but low-paying, support jobs. Extensive oral interviews of both blacks and whites who worked there during the period added the human dimension to the research data and revealed the tremendous gulf between America's promise of equality and the reality, even within the federal bureaucracy.

The exhaustive interviews conducted for this book also include testimonies to the changes that occurred within the Agency, reflective of progress after President Truman's February 1948 message to Congress on civil rights and the issuance of Executive Order 9981 later that year which mandated the integration of the armed services. The book closes in 1956 as NSA is reorganizing and relocating to Fort Meade, Maryland. As part of the reorganization, a large, predominantly black organization, one of the most visible symbols of racial division within the Agency, was dismantled. Thus ended a major chapter in the Agency's social history, but for years afterward, issues of fairness and equality would continue to be at the forefront of the consciousness of many African-Americans at the National Security Agency.

Though thirteen million American Negroes have more often than not been denied democracy, they are American citizens and will as in every war give unqualified support to the protection of their country. At the same time we shall not abate one iota our struggle for full citizenship rights here in the United States. We will fight but we demand the right to fight as equals in every branch of military, naval and aviation service. – From minutes of NAACP Board of Directors meeting, 8 December 1941[1]

The African-American experience at Arlington Hall Station (AHS), home of the National Security Agency and its Army predecessor organizations from 1942 to the mid-fifties, was shaped by a complex set of forces. In the simplest terms, African-American employment, as was that of individuals in any other group, was dictated by the intelligence needs of the nation's political and military leaders. The volume of target communications to be exploited that would provide the needed information and the systems available to process the data translated into manpower requirements. The nature of that employment, however, and the surrounding cultural environment reflected broader issues – the racial policies of the U.S. Army and the state of racial integration in America at large.

Although, to its credit, the racially integrated U.S. Army of the mid-fifties was a decade ahead of most civilian institutions on civil rights issues, the army of the early forties was viciously Jim Crow:

> . . . The policy of the War department is not to intermingle colored and white personnel in the same regimental organizations. This policy has been proven satisfactory over a long period of years and to make

changes would produce situations destructive to morale and detrimental to the preparations for national defense. – Memo from Robert P. Patterson, Assistant Secretary of War, to President Roosevelt, 27 September 1940[2]

In December 1941, nearly 100,000 African-Americans were serving in the racially segregated U.S. Army, the vast majority in infantry, engineering, and quartermaster units. Less than 2 percent of enlistees were in the Signal Corps, and over the next seven months that percentage declined to less than 1 percent.[3] The basis for the Army position on African-American integration[4] was threefold. The two most commonly cited reasons were that the Army reflected the desires of the American people and was not an instrument for social change, and that it was efficient to use personnel according to their skills and capabilities. General George C. Marshall, Army chief of staff, articulated these arguments in a 1 December 1941 memorandum to Secretary of War Henry Stimson:

> The problems presented with reference to utilizing Negro personnel in the army should be faced squarely. In doing so, the following facts must be recognized: first that the War Department cannot ignore the social relationship between Negroes and whites which has been established by the American people through custom and habit; second, that either through lack of educational opportunities or other causes the level of intelligence and occupational skill of the Negro population is considerably below that of the white; third, that the army will attain its maximum strength only if its personnel is [sic] properly placed in accordance with the capabilities of individuals; and fourth, that experiments within the army in the solution of

social problems are fraught with danger to efficiency, discipline, and morale.[5]

"... *the level of intelligence and occupational skill of the Negro population is considerably below that of the white.*" The third plank underpinning the Army's rigid segregationist policies was the belief that African-Americans were inferior. An Army War College (AWC) study published in October 1925 concluded that "the black man was physically unqualified for combat duty; was by nature subservient, mentally inferior, and believed himself to be inferior to the white man; was susceptible to the influence of crowd psychology; could not control himself in the face of danger; and did not have the initiative and resourcefulness of the white man." [6]

Twelve years later, a similar "study" purported to present the Negro personality characteristics that commanders were likely to meet: "As an individual the negro is docile, tractable, lighthearted, care free and good-natured. If unjustly treated he is likely to become surly and stubborn, though this is usually a temporary phase. He is careless, shiftless, irresponsible and secretive. He resents censure and is best handled with praise and by ridicule. He is unmoral, untruthful and his sense of right doing is relatively inferior." [7]

The significance of these and other AWC studies cannot be underestimated. Historian Alan Osur concluded that the 1925 study "establishes the impact of racism upon the minds of these field grade officers of the 1920s who, generally speaking, would become the commanders in World War II. The importance of their early learning cannot be overstated in understanding their subsequent behavior." [8]

Clarence Toomer, an African-American NSA retiree, was a young Army enlistee in 1942. Interviewed in January 2000, he recalled his personal experience with army mandated segregation during World War II:

I grew up and went to school in Fayetteville, North Carolina. After the third year of high school, I decided that I wanted to see the world and I went off and joined the army. This was in 1942.

I was in the Quartermaster Corps. It's transportation now. We moved trucks and supplies or anything that had to be moved. It was an all-black regiment except for the officers. We first went to the West Coast, then we were shipped to Australia. In fact, I was on the maiden voyage of the *Queen Elizabeth*. They brought the ship to San Francisco to protect it from being damaged by the Germans while it was still under construction. Then they converted it to a troop ship. We had 10,000 troops on that ship, stacked four high in elaborate cabins which had forty people in them. It took thirty-nine days to zigzag across the Pacific.

You hear all kinds of stories about Australians not liking blacks, but the citizens were cordial. They received us with open arms. The people in Melbourne had Sunday teas in their homes and churches and would invite the black troops, and we went. They also had skating rinks in the city, but the white Americans identified a recreation area for black troops only. The American government, the American military did that – not the Australians.

Of course, the Army was right about one thing; it did largely reflect civilian attitudes. Schools, housing, restaurants, hotels, movie theaters, and recreational facilities were legally segregated by race in much of the country. Carl Dodd, the grandson of slaves, was a War Department messenger and clerk for approximately six years before joining the Army Security Agency, an NSA forerunner, in

1948. He vividly remembers the discrimination and intimidation endured by blacks in rural North Carolina during the Depression:

> I grew up poor in Smithville. I went to school many days in coveralls and bare feet, and my parents couldn't afford to buy books. In North Carolina, they didn't furnish [blacks with] books until somewhere around 1936 or 1937. Of course, the schools were segregated. Some black kids could buy books, but many couldn't. I used to borrow books from my classmates during activity periods and read in the library. There was a large family of us and we just couldn't do things. We owned our land and home. That's it. My daddy sold a tremendous amount of land during the '30s trying to survive. Nobody worked much but my dad, and he was born of a slave parent. When I speak about him, it hurts me. He couldn't read or write, but he wanted his kids to get an education. We got what we could.

> I came to Washington in 1941, because the Ku Klux Klan activity was terrible, and I had many, many fights with white people. My uncle was hit by a car, and I still don't understand it. An automobile at that time, mostly an A-model Ford or a T-model Ford, came by maybe every thirty minutes. So he had to have been put in front of a car and then hit. Many blacks were killed, and nobody ever knew and nobody ever cared. My mother and father thought it best that I leave. I was seventeen years old.[9]

The African-American press and civil rights organizations pressed the Roosevelt administration, the military, and the nation's political parties for change. The contradiction between an America at war against fascism abroad while inflicting racial injustices on its citizens at home was inescapable. This national struggle over equality became the impetus for a sea change in the employment of African-Americans at AHS.

German Army Attacks Poland;
Cities Bombed

Havas, French news agency, announced that a German declaration of war against Poland probably will lead France and Great Britain to take new military measures. Britain and France are committed to aid Poland in any fight to save her independence. – *New York Times*, September 1, 1939

At the outbreak of the war in Europe in 1939, the Signals Intelligence Service (SIS),[10] the fledgling U.S. cryptologic organization, had been in existence less than ten years. Created in 1930 in the Army's Office of the Chief Signal Officer (OCSigO), it represented the consolidation of the missions of two post-WWI organizations. First, the SIS was to develop secure codes for U.S. military communications (communications security or COMSEC), formerly the responsibility of the Code and Cipher Section in the OCSigO. During wartime, it was also to intercept and solve enemy code and cipher messages (communications intelligence or COMINT), a role that had been assigned to the Cipher Bureau (MI-8) of the General Staff during WWI and continued primarily as a training mission after demobilization. At its formation, William F. Friedman, the Army's foremost cryptologist in the Code and Cipher Section, was named to lead the new organization. After hiring a secretary, Miss Louise Newkirk, he acquired four "junior cryptanalysts" – three mathematicians – Frank Rowlett, Abe Sinkov, and Solomon Kullback, and a Japanese linguist, John Hurt. Added to this small contingent during that first year were an Army officer, Captain Norman Lee Baldwin, whose job would be to establish the Second Signal Service Company, the intercept division of SIS; Lieutenant Mark Rhodes, a Signal Corps officer; and Larry Clark, a chemistry

major who would analyze secret inks. These few individuals comprised the SIS in December 1930.[11]

In his account of the history of the SIS, William Friedman was unequivocal about the initial basis of the small organization's cryptanalytic activities. Interception and decoding of foreign communications were to be undertaken as training in preparation for the execution of its wartime mission, not as peacetime activities. Particularly interesting information uncovered as a by-product of this training would be shown to the Army Assistant Chief of Staff, G2, but there was not a functioning peacetime mission to actively collect and exploit the communications of targeted foreign governments.[12] It was in the execution of this training mission during the mid-1930s, however, that SIS made an indelible impression on senior War Department officials and paved the way for its future expansion. By 1933, the monitoring stations in Fort Monmouth, New Jersey, and at the Presidio in San Francisco were regularly providing intercepts of Japanese diplomatic communications (commonly referred to as "traffic"), the War Department's highest priority intelligence target. In 1936, the SIS, chiefly Frank Rowlett, broke the Japanese diplomatic code generated by the "Red" machine and used for their most sensitive communications. The recovered plaintext messages gave the nation's policy makers and military leaders unprecedented insight into the developing political ties between Japan, Germany, and Italy.

Thus, although fewer than twenty people comprised the SIS in mid-1939, it had established its value to the national leadership and plans existed for both gradual, modest, peacetime growth and contingency expansion during a national emergency. Eleven days after Hitler's army goose-stepped into Poland, the Chief Signal Officer recommended that funds be released for the acquisition of twenty-five additional civilians and more equipment in preparation for implementing its wartime mission. This was soon revised to reflect a request for funds for expansion, to include funds for twenty-six (rather than twenty-five) additional civilians. The final recommendation was approved, and by the end of the year expansion of the SIS professional force of cryptologists and linguists had begun.[13]

Although neither reflected in the War Department authorization letter nor noted in the histories, the tiny secret agency was increased by at least one other employee in late 1939.

Bernard Pryor
(later photo)

On 13 November, Bernard W. Pryor, a thirty-nine-year-old former motorcycle messenger for the Navy Department, entered on duty as the SIS messenger. Almost certainly he was the first African American to be hired at the agency.[14]

> "In 1938, of the 9,717 Negroes regularly employed by the federal government in Washington, 90 percent held custodial jobs for which the top annual pay rate was $1,260; only 9.5 percent had clerical jobs, and only 47 men had subprofessional rank."[15]

*   *   *   *

> "The population of the metropolitan [Washington, D.C.] area mushroomed from 621,000 in 1930 to well over a million by the end of 1941. Seventy thousand new people arrived in the first year after Pearl Harbor alone. Government employment had more than doubled since the beginning of 1940, and more than five thousand new federal workers were pouring into Washington every month, often bringing their families with them."

David Brinkley, *Washington Goes To War* (New York, NY, 1988), 107

SIS personnel authorizations, by July 1942, had increased to 364 civilians and 121 officers.[16] Already desperately short of space at the Munitions Building, but still expanding to support the war effort, the Army purchased a women's junior college at 4000 Lee Boulevard, Arlington, Virginia, for the burgeoning agency. The new location had an added advantage. The now vital SIS would be removed from downtown Washington where it was believed it was more vulnerable to enemy bombing or agent activity.[17] By the end of the summer, most of the agency had relocated to what came to be called Arlington Hall Station (AHS).

Frequently described as a beautiful, campus-like facility, AHS experienced rapid wartime growth. By mid-July 1943, 1,713 civilians, 157 officers, and 240 enlisted personnel[18] were distributed across six sections, most under the direction of a military officer:

Chief, Signal Security Agency
Colonel W. Preston Corderman

Director of Communications Research
Mr. William F. Friedman

A Branch/Protective Security
Major J.C. Sheetz

B Branch/Cryptanalytic
(solution of codes and ciphers)
Lt. Colonel Earle F. Cooke

C Branch/Cryptographic
(communications security)
Colonel Clinton B. Allsopp

D Branch/Laboratory
(secret inks)
Lt. Colonel A.J. McGrail

E Branch/Communications
Lt. Colonel H. McD. Brown

F Branch/Development
Major Leo Rosen

(From Organizational Chart, Signal Security Service, 15 April 1943-1 March 1944 (NSA Archives, Accession No. 18675)).

The larger population of linguists, cryptanalysts, engineers, and mathematicians was reflected in the increased hiring of messengers, probably all of whom were Afro-American. By mid-1943, Bernie Pryor was the senior messenger of fifteen, but one SIS researcher's comments suggest they were stereotyped as "colored" servants of limited intelligence:

> It often happens that translators in distant wings are too remote and hot to bring questions personally. An attempt has been made to improve the situation by utilizing North Carolina messengers. They come, but either have not understood the message or have forgotten it on the way.[19]

*　　*　　*　　*

The nation's capital that drew the new civil servants, both black and white, was a boom town. Seventeen-year-old Carl Dodd was a construction worker in the District of Columbia before becoming a messenger in the Office of the Chief Signal Officer during WWII. In his oral interview, he vividly described the living conditions for many African-American residents during this period of rapid expansion and provided a telling glimpse of the state of civil rights in the capital city as the country entered WWII.

Washington was very, very poor at that time. Where the Pentagon building is, there used to be a Hot Shoppe and an airfield. There was a 'colored' area right near there called Queen City. The Pentagon took all the property these people had. Then they built houses for the people that they had thrown out. That is when I saw the first low income housing – off of Columbia Pike, near Arlington – right near the Navy Department. It was called Johnson Hill. The people had to have some place to live; however, some of these buildings were like shanties, and they had cesspools – no plumbing. But it was their homes. You can't pay somebody $200 or $250 for a house and replace it for that amount of money, but that's what the government did. Just like they did in southwest [District of Columbia]. Many of those houses in southwest had no plumbing. They had a big truck to come around and pick up the sewage from the houses in big buckets. They used to call it the 'honey wagon', and you could smell it for blocks.

People lived wherever they could get low rent. When I first came to Washington [in 1941], I lived in a room on Fairfax Drive, and I got a job doing construction work. I paid $3.50 a week for my room, and I got $7.00 a week as a salary. When I went into the government in 1942, I was hired as a CU [custodial] 3 [$1,200 per year]. After taxes, I took home $42 every two weeks. So I had clothes, rent, food – everything to take care of. I had nothing left. Things weren't good, but a lot of black people came to Washington thinking things were much better than they really were.

My first government job in 1942 was as a messenger for the Office of the Chief Signal Officer, and I was at the Munitions Building at 2nd and T Street, Southwest [District of Columbia]. At that time, the cafeteria was segregated. I think it was desegregated about the same time as the Pentagon was completed. Roosevelt ordered that there would be no more segregation in the cafeteria. Prior to then, we could not go into it. They had little cubby holes in the back where you could go and get food, if you wanted, but I didn't go there. I went to a place on the wharf called Benny Bordnick's. We couldn't go in there and sit down either, but we could buy their fish sandwiches, crabcakes, or whatever we wanted and take it back. We got a good buy, and we got good food. There was another place called Cadillac, a black place, but we always went to Benny Bordnick's and brought our food back.

*   *   *   *

In early 1944, Colonel W. Preston Corderman, a 1926 West Point graduate from Hagerstown, Maryland, was chief of what was then being called the Signal Security Agency. Earle F. Cooke, who once headed the COMSEC side of the agency (C Branch), was chief of the cryptanalysis effort (B Branch). Interviewed years later, General Cooke described a pivotal conversation between the two that led to the creation of a segregated unit of black cryptologists at AHS.

Eleanor Roosevelt, through her channels . . . had the Signal Corps advise that . . . twelve percent or fifteen percent of our personnel had to be black and gainfully employed. A problem. We had one who was a mes-

senger. I can't remember his name. Racked my brain and I can't remember it. Anyway, the problem was, what do we do now, because here we have a directive and we're going to have to put a lot of black people to work. We decided, I guess I did, because Corderman said to me,'Your job. I'm not going to have them on any other staff. I'm going to have them on your staff, okay?' The problem [was] what to do and I decided I'm going to keep this bunch as a unit and find something which they can do worthwhile. The only help I had in selecting black personnel was this messenger. Well, I liked the guy. He was a good guy, and he was a hard-working guy and I told him I got this problem. I got to have about a hundred and some odd people of your race ('niggers' in that day), and I says, you're my personnel officer to see that I get the right ones. Did a marvelous job. Where the hell he got them and how he got them, I knew not. I put him in touch with the personnel people and said, that guy is my representative in hiring these people. Your job is to hire them when he says so. And he did. I haven't the slightest idea [what criteria he used], but we gave them some stuff working on some Allied system. I don't know what system we had them on. . . . It doesn't matter. The output, of course, was more or less negative . . . but so what? We had the unit, had no problem.[20]

Lt. Col. Earle Cooke

[*Editor's Note: There is no actual documentation that Mrs. Roosevelt ordered the hiring of African-Americans either in the Signal Corps or at AHS. Given the nature of the social picture at the time, however, such actions needed the intervention of "someone in a high place."*]

The messenger whose name General Cooke could no longer recall was William (Bill) Coffee, once a houseman and waiter at the Arlington Hall School for Girls, who was then working for Bernie Pryor. Born in Abingdon, Virginia, in 1917, Mr. Coffee studied English at Knoxville College, Tennessee, in 1936 after attending the Kings Mountain Training School in Abingdon. During the closing years of the Depression, from 1937 to 1940, he was enrolled in the Civilian Conservation Corps. Thereafter followed a series of jobs as a waiter, before he was hired in September 1941 by the Arlington Hall School for Girls. When the Army acquired the property, Mr. Coffee applied for a federal position and was hired as a junior janitor for the SIS in June 1942, eventually being promoted to messenger. In January 1944, after Earle F. Cooke tapped him to satisfy Mrs. Roosevelt's concerns, he set about building a unit that would be "gainfully employed." His job title was officially changed to cryptographic clerk in June of that year, and an organizational chart dated 15 November 1944 identified him as Assistant Civilian In Charge of B-3-b, with nineteen subordinate civilians.[21] Their mission was not the analysis of Allied codes, as General Cooke recalled, but the exploitation of commercial coded messages. Several military officers very briefly served as chief of the unit before the position was assumed by Benson K. Buffham in mid-1944, who held it first as a young military officer, then as a civilian, until February 1947.

yeqyx ipeoa ipeco caozr ivmzi oatab

_ _ _ _ _ _ _ _ _ _ _ _ _ _ _

(Pineapple must be packed very carefully. Mark outside of packages plainly, with gross and net weights. Customers will pay for cost of transshipment. Telegraph us at time shipment is made.)

orutl yeqyx oczom

_ _ _ _ _ _ _ _ _ _ _ _ _ _

(In accordance with your telegram, pineapple will be shipped immediately.) – English texts and commercial code equivalents from *Acme Commodity and Phrase Code*, New York, 1923

Very quickly after the introduction of the American Morse code for telegraphic messages, it was recognized that this new mode of communicating seriously threatened privacy. Inserted between the originator and intended recipient of the information were persons who would translate it into the Morse symbols and key the message and other individuals to receive the message and render it readable for the recipient. The most sensitive data would, therefore, be accessible to these middlemen. Thus, in 1845 an associate of Samuel Morse published a code for Morse communications, "The Secret Corresponding Vocabulary; Adapted for Use to Morse's Electro-Magnetic Telegraph," to provide the message originator with a means of securing correspondence.

As telegraph usage grew in the late 1840s and 1850s, other codes for Morse communications appeared, but it was the laying of the first transatlantic cable in 1866 that sparked an explosion of codes for Morse communications. The driver for this creativity was not secrecy, but economy, for the telegraph companies charged by the word, as well as according to the distance between the sender and the receiver. Consequently, the economies offered by the shorthand codes, which became known as "commercial codes," were extremely attractive. Scores of industries developed lexicons that could, with a simple group of letters, convey multiple phrases or sentences.[22] During WWII, the information transmitted by foreign companies by this means was of interest to U.S. officials, since it could provide trade and travel data and some insight into the economic conditions of the companies' host nations.

An SIS unit of four people, all Caucasians, was actively exploiting foreign commercial coded messages as early as February 1943. By May there were six, and in September 1943 eight people comprised B-2a-8, the Commercial Unit in the Code Recovery Section of the Cryptanalytic Branch. The unit was headed by a succession of junior Army officers in the fall of 1943, but gradually the personnel were transferred to other higher priority tasks, and by December 1943 the mission was completely abandoned.[23] It was a situation tailor-made for the moment. No Caucasians were working the problem, obviating the need to address the issue of an integrated work unit. Clearly the work was meaningful, but if no results were produced, it would only be a continuation of the status quo for the customers. On the other hand, if the unit proved productive, the results could be useful. Mrs. Roosevelt's requirements could be met.

In January 1944, Bill Coffee started his new assignment as a cryptographic clerk. Undoubtedly he underwent some cryptanalytic training, but a record of courses that he might have taken at the time is no longer available. Initially he worked alone; then in February 1944 Annie Briggs, who had worked with him in the messenger unit, joined him as his assistant.[24] The unit grew in size and, though clearly an operational unit with core mission responsibilities, for several months it was retained as a staff element reporting to the chief of the Cryptanalytic Branch, consistent with Corderman's direction to Cooke. A memorandum announcing one of the many Signal Security Agency reorganizations alluded to this inconsistency:

> Effective 21 August [1944], the Intelligence Division [formerly the Cryptanalytic Branch or B Branch] was organized to consist of an Office of the Division Chief and five operating branches. . . . The Commercial Traffic Section has, for reasons of policy, been retained under the control of the Division Chief instead of being absorbed into the General Cryptanalytic Branch [one of the five subordinate branches of the Intelligence Division], which might normally appear to be its proper location.[25]

Eventually, however, logic prevailed. By mid-November 1944, the unit became part of the General Cryptanalytic Branch, which was headed by Lieutenant Colonel Frank B. Rowlett, one of the four original cryptanalysts hired by William Friedman. Its designator became B-3-b. The organizational chart reflects Lieutenant Benson K. Buffham as the chief and William D. Coffee, assistant civilian in charge.[26]

*   *   *   *

B-3-b, under Lieutenant Buffham and Bill Coffee, exploited nongovernmental commercial code messages originating from Australia, Great Britain, Germany, Sweden, Spain, Portugal, Bulgaria, Turkey, Afghanistan, Russia, China, Indochina, Thailand, Japan, Egypt, South Africa, Ecuador, Uruguay, Paraguay, Brazil, Peru, and Argentina.[27]

Conventional intercept sources and the Office of Censorship, which under the War Powers Act received copies of all cable traffic from the U.S. carriers, supplied the raw material (messages) for the unit. Communications using both private codes and codes available on the open market were decoded. Messages that were found to be written in an unknown commercial code or in an enciphered commercial code, i.e., individual letters of the code phrase were substituted or transposed, were analyzed to identify the underlying codebook and ultimately to recover the plain text. Additionally, the unit sorted and routed nongovernmental Spanish, French, Italian, Portuguese, German, and English plaintext messages, a task that formerly had been accomplished by the Traffic Unit.[28]

This work was accomplished by three sections. The largest, Production, led by Annie Briggs, identified codes, decoded messages, and provided clerical support. Ethel Just headed a small group of translators in the Language unit. Herman Phynes directed the last section, the B-3-b technical element charged with solving encipherments. Twenty-eight years into the future, Herman Phynes would be a GG-16, army flag officer equivalent, and NSA's first African-American office chief in the

Herman Phynes
(later photo)

Operations Directorate. In March 1944, however, he was a subprofessional (SP)-5 cryptanalytic aide returning to government work after brief stints as an insurance salesman and a real estate agent. A Washington, D.C., native, he was a graduate of Dunbar High School and had a B.A. degree (1941) from Howard University. His earlier government service was as a clerk for the Internal Revenue Service and as a messenger and clerk in the War Department, but dissatisfied with both the pay and levels of responsibility, he left the civil service to seek work more consistent with his academic background.[29]

One other significant personnel change occurred in 1944. Bernie Pryor, the messenger for the Signals Intelligence Service, was reassigned in April 1944 to the Personnel Branch as a clerk. Undoubtedly, with the anticipation of increased hiring of African-Americans came the realization that this segment of the workforce would require support services. He thus became a human resources unit for black employees, providing a variety of employee services, including orientation briefings, information on housing and recreational facilities, and counseling on work, family, and personal financial matters.[30]

* * * *

Benson K. Buffham, the administrative chief of B-3-b, had entered the Signal Corps in 1942, one year after graduating from Wesleyan University (Connecticut). In June 1999, he looked back nearly sixty years and recounted his first days at Arlington Hall and his early assignment as head of the first group of African-American cryptologists.

Benson K. Buffham

When I first went to Arlington Hall, I worked as a cryptanalyst (or cryppie) for about six months, working Japanese diplomatic communications. Then, a very good friend of mine at the time, Captain Mike Maloney, who was Frank Rowlett's plans and priorities officer,[31] was assigned overseas, and he recommended to Colonel Rowlett that I replace him. So I became the plans and priorities officer on the staff of B3. It was then that I was also assigned, as one of my duties, the job with the just emerging black unit. Maloney had that job before me, and when I replaced him I took that job as well. I was introduced to Bill Coffee and became the head of the unit; however, Coffee was really the operating head of the unit. I had other jobs to do at the same time. He was full-time in that job, and he was really the expert. I was the reporting chain for them, so Coffee reported to me, and I got all of his reports and reviewed them. I wouldn't say that I reviewed them all before they went out, but if they thought they had anything really significant, Coffee would show it to me first.

I was located maybe a hundred yards away from Coffee's area at a desk outside Colonel Rowlett's office. There were maybe fifteen or so people on the staff, including his secretary and personnel people. I didn't have an office. The B-3-b unit was in a separate room. Colonel Rowlett was very interested in the unit and would visit them from time to time. Bill Coffee sat right at the head and was really in charge of that area. At the time, we had a large number of black Americans working in what I would call custodial type jobs at Arlington Hall, but Mr. Coffee's unit was the only professional unit that I'm aware of.

We had the Office of Censorship in World War II, and one of my jobs was to go down to Censorship every day and collect the international material which was flowing through them, but which they weren't processing. They were only interested in things originating in or destined for the United States. Everything had to be filed with them, and they would examine material that was coming in or out of the U.S., but they wouldn't be able to examine material that was going from Tokyo, for example, to a number of foreign cities. That [international] material all fell within the realm of responsibility of the SIS. All that material had to be examined by our commercial code unit.

They [B-3-b analysts] were responsible for detecting anything that would be transpiring which wasn't routine trade. Of course there was a great deal of traffic, because we were monitoring all the international communications, particularly from Tokyo and Berlin – all the enemy traffic. But, it all had to be gone through, because you had to be sure that we weren't missing something that would be a violation of the international embargoes. Although item for item, it wasn't as important as diplomatic traffic, they performed an invaluable service by going through all that material and making sure there wasn't anything in it that would have been useful for us in the wartime effort.[32]

*   *   *   *

For several months, B-3-b continued to expand in mission and resources under Bill Coffee. In April 1945, it was assigned responsibility for exploiting the diplomatic systems of Belgium, Haiti, Liberia,

and Luxembourg, though there is no evidence that this mission developed past the research stage. By June, Bill Coffee was directing the efforts of thirty people distributed over six sections, plus a secretary. Most were engaged in the major activities of code identification and decoding; researching and analyzing unknown codes; and translating.[33]

Major international trade activity resumed following the end of WWII with a concomitant substantial rise in the volume of commercial coded messages, but agency postwar personnel losses were reflected in the sharply reduced manning of B-3-b (renamed WDGAS-93K when the Signals Security Division became the Army Security Agency in September 1945). In July 1946, it was composed of fewer than a dozen people.

In February 1946, Bill Coffee was transferred to the Intercept Control Branch as the supervisor of a new typing unit which had been formed to augment the automatic morse transcription section of nearby Vint Hill Farms in Warrenton, Virginia. In the two years that he was associated with the Commercial Code unit, he had advanced from a CAF-3 ($1,620/year) to a CAF-5 ($2,430/year).[34] Replacing him as assistant O.I.C. (officer in charge) of the African-American commercial code cryptologists was his principal assistant, Herman Phynes.

On 3 April 1946, General W. Preston Corderman, chief, Army Security Agency, presented William D. Coffee with the prestigious Commendation for Meritorious Civilian Service.

In February 1947, the practice of having a Caucasian as the nominal head of the Commercial Code unit ended with the appointment of Herman Phynes to the position of O.I.C. He was a P-2 (Professional Level -2) with an annual salary of $3,522.60.[35]

William Coffee receiving the Meritorious Service Award
from General W. Preston Corderman, Chief, ASA,
3 April 1946

Although B-3-b was a unique and unprecedented organization, these early African-American cryptanalysts and translators appear to have been virtually invisible. Few former Agency employees who were interviewed and who worked at AHS during WWII had any knowledge of African-Americans in professional positions; most did not even recall seeing African-Americans on the campus.

*   *   *   *

From Stettin in the Baltic to Trieste in the Adriatic, an iron curtain has descended across the Continent. Behind that line lie all the capitals of the ancient states of Central and Eastern Europe. – Winston Churchill at Westminster College, Fulton, Missouri, 5 March 1946

The Soviet Union – the military intentions of its leaders, the success of its espionage efforts, the status of its advanced weapons and nuclear programs, and the globalization of its political ideology – dominated the American national psyche in the decades after WWII. The intelligence needs of the U.S. and its closest allies translated into manpower requirements which, in the late 1940s to mid-1950s, were particularly acute at the GG-2/GG-3 level. Hiring of African-Americans rose dramatically, and by the early 1950s large concentrations existed in two areas of the Operations organization: machine processing (specifically, equipment operations and keypunch) and Russian plaintext processing. Among people of color, these areas came to be known as "Little Africa," "the hole," "the plantation," and "the snakepit."

* * * *

William Friedman is credited with introducing IBM equipment to the Signals Intelligence Service in 1935 for the compilation of War Department codes. The initial acquisition consisted of a key punch (to record the plain text that was to be encoded and the corresponding code groups); a sorter (to randomize the punched cards); and a printing tabulator. Not long after the machines were acquired, however, their utility to cryptanalysis was recognized. They became the tools to manipulate intercepted code groups and to perform exhaustive searches, frequency counts, compar-

isons, and statistical computations in the effort to uncover the underlying plain text. Initially Friedman's cryptanalysts operated the equipment, but this proved inefficient as additional equipment and personnel were acquired. In October 1939, two full-time experienced key punchers were hired, and the policy of training cryptanalysts on IBM equipment was discontinued. In December 1939, Ulrich Kropfl, a tabulating equipment operator from the new Social Security Administration, joined SIS and became the first chief of the machine section.[36]

One of the early members of the new section was Norm Willis, a 1942 graduate of McKinley High School in Washington, D.C., who entered on duty as a tabulating equipment operator. Interviewed in 1999, Mr. Willis described his early assignment sorting Japanese army traffic and the section's racial composition during the war years:

> There were intercept operators in the field, in Europe and in the Pacific, and they would intercept messages and would write them by hand. They then would somehow ship them back to the States, so you know by the time they arrived here, it was not time sensitive. The messages would come in, and we had a group of key punch operators, mostly girls, but some military men as well, who would put them in card form. Then they would be edited, and once they were accurate they might be listed or batched in certain ways, according to the needs of the intelligence analyst. I was an operator on the midnight shift. We handled Japanese traffic, and I was responsible for making sure that the cards were accurately punched from the traffic. For most of WWII, that is what I did, and the only black was a man named Bill Williams. He was custodial, but he also worked in

supply. In other words, to punch cards, you had to buy these sixty-pound cartons of cards, five boxes of two thousand cards each. IBM would ship them in, and Bill Williams handled the unloading and loading, but there were no blacks at all in the machine section during WWII.[37]

Delores Schommer, one of the Agency's first key punch operators, was initially hired in 1936 for the new Social Security Administration. It was there that she met Ulrich Kropfl, whom William Friedman selected in 1939 to head up the machine section. Upon his recommendation, in July 1940 Mrs. Schommer transferred to SIS as a key punch operator. Although wartime requirements necessitated additional personnel, she too indicated the machine section was not integrated until later in the 1940s.

> Before the war, we had huge tabulators, and men like Sam Snyder, Larry Clark, and Dr. Kullback, testing out this new equipment to see what it could do.[38] It was all very new. I know Ulrich wanted to get another tabulator, and he talked with General Akin about this. General Akin kinda huffed and finally ordered it, but it took quite a while to get it. Soon, I had three girls working with me. We decided to hire some more, so we hired five or six more who came to work at night. We were in a little room, probably not much bigger than 16 feet x 18 feet. Then the war came, and we needed to expand. They bought Arlington Hall, and built two buildings – A Building and B Building – and we moved on Thanksgiving Day of '42. I'm not sure when the first blacks came, but Geneva Arthur was one of the early ones.[39]

The year that the machine section first employed African-Americans cannot be pinpointed. Though both Norm Willis and Delores Schommer claim there were no blacks in the unit during WWII, Mr. Willis recalls seeing, "sometime early on," Alton B. Dunkinson, a technician who would "help in the development of special hardware that you connected to the IBM equipment." According to David Shepard, who arrived at SIS in 1944, "Tony" Dunkinson, once a signal man for the New York City subway system, was already there. His career with the agency, however, lasted only into the early fifties when he left to become an engineer at a systems development company formed by Mr. Shepard.[40]

The major influx of African-Americans into the machine section seems to have begun in 1947. Geneva Arthur, remembered by Delores Schommer as "one of the early ones," entered on duty, with several others, in December of that year.

> "Most of the civilians that were hired during World War II were from North Carolina, Virginia, and the South. These were white, a lot of them young girls right out of high school. They did not have a history of eating with people of color. I don't know when it was, but one day, in the cafeteria there was one of the other white workers eating lunch with [a black man]. That took nerve in that time. It took courage for the guy who was doing that because of the social environment."
>
> Norm Willis, 11 January 1999

Geneva Arthur entered on duty at the Army Security Agency in December 1947 and spent her entire career in the key punch unit, retiring in 1973 as a section head. According to her, the key punch unit was always integrated, whites and African-Americans holding both supervisory and nonsupervisory positions.[41] Documentation on the changes in the demographics of the machine section is unavailable, but most retirees formerly assigned there supported this view only with qualification. They claim that while in the mid- to late 1940s the organization was integrated, by the mid-fifties civilian African-Americans overwhelmingly dominated in nonsupervisory positions in the key punch and tabulating equipment units. Repeatedly, the perception was voiced that the relatively few white civilians who were assigned to entry-level positions in the organization eventually were either promoted to successively higher supervisory positions or transferred to other parts of the Agency.

* * * *

The ASA effort to exploit Russian plaintext traffic began in 1946 with the part-time assignment of several linguists to the target. At that time, however, the Agency's emphasis was on the translation of encrypted messages, and the employment of scarce Russian linguists on plain text was judged to be unwarranted. Later, in May 1947, the effort was revised at the Pentagon. Individuals without security clearances or with partial clearances would sift through volumes of messages and translate all or parts of those determined to have intelligence value. Placed in charge of this group was Jacob Gurin, an ASA Russian linguist who had immigrated to the U.S. with his parents at the age of three. A graduate of New York University, "Jack" grew up in a Russian-speaking household and spoke the language fluently. During the war, he served as a Japanese linguist for the U.S. Army, and after discharge, applied to the Army Security Agency. In 1946, native-speaking Russian language ability was a valuable and rare commodity. Security concerns arising from his birthplace were resolved, and he joined the organization as a Russian linguist. Within months of his entry on duty, he engineered a revolutionary approach to the exploitation and reporting of Russian plaintext communications.[42]

From the Agency's inception under William Friedman, its business was the breaking of codes and ciphers. Once the underlying text was revealed, individual messages were translated, and, after a reporting mission was established, selected ones were published on 3" x 5" cards. While individual decrypted messages could be extremely valuable, plaintext messages were most often preformatted status reports that were insignificant when considered singly. Jack Gurin was convinced that if these messages were assembled and analyzed in the aggregate, they could yield valuable information on Soviet defense capabilities. Initially, three linguists were assigned to him plus a writer/editor. Their task was to select messages that qualified for immediate translation and publication or which could be used in a research report on a subject of interest. Much of the intercept data was passed to the linguists by a group of processing personnel who would provide page print-outs of material that had been sent to the agency on tape. The tape conversion process involved running a paper tape of radioprinter signals through a machine (the CXCO tape printer) which read coded perforations and printed the corresponding Cyrillic characters. It was a repetitive, manual task requiring minimal cognitive skills and initially was accomplished by a small number of whites, who gradually transferred out of the positions. According to Agency retiree Dave Bryant, he and fourteen other African-Americans transferred to ASA from the Census Bureau in 1947. They were assigned to this traffic processing unit, and from this small cadre of black communications clerks grew a large, essentially all-black division in the Operations Directorate of NSA.[43]

Jacob Gurin
(later photo)

CXCO tape printer

David Bryant, one of the original African-
American employees in the Russian plaintext
traffic processing unit. (later photo)

The development and expansion of the traffic processing unit are inextricably linked to the tremendous dependence on the exploitation of Russian communications for intelligence following Black Friday. That day, 25 August 1948, the chief of the Soviet General Staff declared that "the transmission of . . . messages is permitted only by landline." Within weeks, Soviet communications systems that had been successfully exploited since 1945 went off the air. The series of communications changes that began in November 1947 and culminated on Black Friday were catastrophic. Out of this devastation, Russian plaintext communications emerged as the critical provider of intelligence on our primary Cold War adversary.[44]

Eighteen months after Black Friday, in March 1950, the chairman of the United States Communication Intelligence Board (USCIB) Intelligence Committee wrote that Soviet plaintext traffic could, at least partially, fulfill two vital intelligence requirements: (a) Soviet intentions to make war and (b) Soviet capabilities to make war. Accordingly, the Armed Forces Security Agency (AFSA), as the agency was then named, was requested to accomplish complete processing of traffic.[45] By July 1950, over a million messages a month were being forwarded to AFSA for processing and exploitation. The plaintext exploitation unit stood at 170, and it was projected that by April 1952, the volume of messages requiring processing would nearly double, requiring an additional 350 people.[46] During the 1950/1951 time frame, Russian plain text was nearing its zenith in terms of intelligence priorities, collection resources, and personnel; and AFSA-213,[47] the all-black traffic processing branch (later a division) that came to be known as "the snakepit," "the plantation," and "the black hole of Calcutta," was in full operation.

All Russian plaintext traffic forwarded to Arlington Hall Station from U.S. sources was received in AFSA-213. In mid-1950, a paper delivered to Captain Mason (AFSA-02, Chief of Operations), entitled the "Russian Plain Text Problem," placed the AFSA-213 manning at 98 and projected the 1952 personnel requirement at 218. The paper also supplied a concise, descriptive account of the work performed in the traffic processing branch:

> **The incoming material is of two types, printed messages and perforated radio printer tapes. The printed messages result from the collection of either . . . radio printer communications that were intercepted using standard teletype equipment or . . . morse transmissions that were transcribed from undulator tape recordings.**
> **. . . radio printer communications are recorded and printed on perforated teletype tapes in the field, and the tapes are forwarded to AFSA for processing.**
>
> **Once the material arrives in the Traffic Division, the employees scan it for key words, addresses, and signatures. Messages that meet the selection criteria are assigned a two-digit routing number that separates them into homogenous groupings. Messages that are on tape are sent to the tape printing section for conversion to hard-copy. The selected, printed messages are then stamped with a one-up serial number and microfilmed. In the final step, they are sent to the sections of the plain text branch, according to the two-digit routing number assigned during the initial scanning process.[48]**

William Jones worked in AFSA-213 from November 1951 until mid-1955. In an oral interview thirty years later, he provided a remarkably similar account of the process, but added the human dimension.

> After I was hired and cleared, I was marched down to the first wing, first floor of A Building and escorted into what was a huge wing, and in there was nothing but black people, except there was an Air Force major in charge of that operation. When you walked in the door, there were long tables, at least twenty feet long, perhaps three and a half/four feet wide, lined up against the wall on both sides of the wing with an aisle down the middle. On each of those tables there must have been eight, possibly ten machines that were like typewriters, except they were printers. They had a little device on the side of them that would read a tape; this was five-level punch paper tape. You put the tape in the reader, start the machine, and the machine would type what was on the tape in hard copy. We only had to type a heading on the page which consisted of basic data like the TO and FROM, the intercept station designator, and the date and time of intercept.

> Well, it didn't take long to pick that operation up. I knew that somewhere people were selecting messages, and I began to wonder how did they pick some messages and throw some away. So as a result, I enrolled in a Russian course at the Department of Agriculture. Soon, I was off the machines and pulling tapes, based on keywords. Once we pulled the tapes, we bundled them in categories and put numbers on them that designated subject areas. But it was a little more complicated than that. Many times the print on the tape was not clear, so we had to read the punched holes. I think what we did was

> critical because we threw away what we thought wasn't any good. If there was anything good in there, it was lost – it went in the burn bag. We were called 'scanners'.

> We heard nothing about career choices or moving to any other place. I went to the Department of Agriculture to take Russian because I didn't know they would teach it here. There were people in that place [AFSA-213] who had degrees, had teaching experience, and a bunch of them had advanced degrees. It was kind of revealing, I think, to ultimately find out that most of the black people who came to the Agency, no matter the kind of experience they had, wound up there.[49]

*   *   *   *

The grade range in AFSA-213 was low. Many, including Dick Hill, who retired as a GG-15 division chief, attested to the fact that new employees entered as a GG-2 or GG-3, despite having a college degree or work experience.

> I was working at the Bureau of Engraving and Printing and had a master's degree in psychology from Howard University. I was looking for better employment, and I submitted an application to the agency. They were hiring, and I was told that I was qualified to come in as a GS-7; however, they didn't have any GS-7 openings at the time. I called back; they still didn't have any openings at a 7 level, but they had some GS-5 openings. I could come in as a 5. I decided that if I was qualified for a GS-7, there was no sense coming in as a 5, and I would wait a little longer. Well, I called and called, and I finally got to the point where I really wanted to get away from the bureau. When I called again, they didn't have any GS-5 openings; they offered me a GS-3, and I accepted. I was hired and sent to whatever that number was – 294 or

what not. It was entirely black with the exception of the division chief. The deputy division chief was a black named Jenkins Johnson. The division chief was an army captain. Not long after I arrived, my section was audited, and all of the jobs were downgraded to GS-2.[50]

Interviewees who worked in AFSA-213 singled out the tape to hard-copy conversion process as mind-numbing and document stamping as both boring and dirty. Further, they revealed that they worked under a production quota system. Scanners were required to review a minimum of 300 messages per day, and page printers were required to print a minimum number of messages. If an employee met the daily quota, his/her name was posted on a board with a star. Monthly statistics were kept, and employees who regularly failed to meet their quotas were counseled.[51] This system of recognition/discipline was taken quite seriously by the subordinates, occasionally with most interesting consequences:

> Boxes of tapes would come in [to AFSA-213], and the only whites you would see were service guys that would bring them in. It was sort of funny, because some of the people that had been scanning for years knew the best tapes, the best links. We were working on quotas, and you wouldn't want to get tapes from the bad links because you wouldn't get anything from them. One lady almost fell in the box of tapes trying to get the best ones.[52]

The monotony of the tasks in AFSA-213 and the underutilization of people were recognized as early as 1948. According to Jack Gurin, founder of the Russian plaintext exploitation branch, it was he who initiated the scanning task in the traffic processing branch. Overwhelmed by the monthly traffic volumes, he sought to reduce the workload on his translators and use them more efficiently.

There was this outfit that took these paper tapes where you couldn't read them unless you could read these little holes. You put them into this machine. You make sure it's all lined up properly, and you press the 'on' button. It starts typing and sheets of printed paper would come out. The equipment was called 'Cxco'. I don't remember what that stands for. These people, as I remembered, were all college graduates; all black and all college graduates. Their job was to sit there and watch the machine and make sure it didn't jam. If it jammed, you stopped the machine and pulled out the keys or fixed the paper. Then you started it again and waited for the next jam. That was their job. I looked at them and said this is ridiculous. They were college graduates. They all have some kind of brains. Since the traffic consisted of official messages, they always had the address. I took all the people in this outfit and taught them the elements of Russian, at least the alphabet. I gave them a sheet that said, this [unit] is number 27, this [unit] is number 29, and so forth. So what they did, as the stuff was coming off, they looked at it and looked at the address and put down the correct number. It wasn't terribly challenging, but it was a lot better than what they were doing before.[53]

Low salaries, monotonous, routine tasks, and limited opportunities for advancement made for poor morale. In the summer of 1953, the Agency's managers sought to mitigate the situation by piping in music.

> Equipment for the reception of music is being installed in the rear of wing 2, first floor, A Building. Since this is considered an area of low personnel morale as a result of recent downgrading and the monotonous work, it is believed the music will be well received.[54]

The music system was never installed. The documentation contains no explanation, but the proposal may have been abandoned because it was impractical. The audio would have had to have been at an ear-piercing level to be heard over the din of a hundred teletype machines.

*   *   *   *

Despite uncomfortable working conditions and dim prospects for change, AFSA-213 employees delivered large quantities of messages to the Russian plaintext exploitation branch every month. Undoubtedly, most were motivated by the simple need to keep their employment. Iris Carr, however, expressed other contributors to her work ethic – pride of accomplishment and, despite the racial discrimination she experienced, patriotism. At the age of thirty-three, she was older than most of the employees in AFSA-213 and was cited by many as being an unheralded hero of the period – one who worked diligently and sought to motivate others.

Iris Carr

When I graduated from Prairie View College [Prairie View, Texas] in 1932, I received a Bachelor of Science degree with a double major, English and math. I taught school, first in a little town, Horton, Texas, and then in Austin. In Texas at that time, the highest level of education you could get was a B.S. or a B.A. degree. There were no other provisions for minorities. You could not go to the University of Texas or to any of the other white colleges. The state of Texas would pay your transportation to go to another school because teachers were required to go to school every three years, but I went every year because I wanted to get another degree. So, several summers I drove from Texas to New York to take courses at Columbia University.

In 1944, I left Austin for Washington because they would not allow blacks to pay into the teacher's retirement fund. I could see myself as a little old lady of sixty or seventy with no income and not able to work. I knew I had to get someplace where I could earn retirement benefits. I also wanted to do something to help out in the war.

My first job was at the Office of the Recorder of Deeds. Then, after the war, schools were opened for veterans and a black electronics school [Hilltop Radio Electronics Institute] on U Street needed teachers. I graded math papers and taught business English in this school for radiomen and electricians. While I was working there I met Bernice Mills, who was working at the agency. She took my application in and shortly after that I was called for an interview.

The work [in AFSA-213] was rather boring, because it was the same thing every day. But if you knew what you were doing and what you were looking for, it was more interesting. We learned to read a Russian dictionary, and we could pick up bits of information on different tapes. From that, you would get an idea of what was going on. If something was completely irrelevant, we would throw it away, but I explained to people that they had to be very careful to give the analysts all the messages we possibly can, because the work was important. . . . Most of the people I worked with were younger than I, and I felt an obligation to be as good as I could be to help them to be good.[55]

Leaders of AFSA-213, ca. 1951.
(Photo courtesy of Clarence Pearson)

The AFSA mission . . . is to provide authentic information for planners and policy makers within the National Military Establishment and other Governmental Agencies having membership on the United States Communication Intelligence Board to apprise them of the realities of the international situation, war-making capabilities, vulnerabilities and intentions of foreign countries, and to eliminate the element of surprise from an act of aggression by another country. – Requirements for Conduct of an Optimum Communication Intelligence Program, 14 July 1950[56]

When armed conflict began in Korea in June 1950, 390 employees (military and civilian) were assigned to the Machine Division.[57] Driven by the Agency's operating philosophy that exhaustive collection and processing of Russian communications and extensive coverage of the communications of Communist China were required to execute its mission, that number rose to 573 in March 1951.[58] Cryptanalysis could be accomplished only through machine manipulation of the data, and as interception capabilities expanded, appropriate increases in processing personnel were required. Hiring of African-Americans to become tabulating equipment operators or key punchers exploded in the early 1950s.

Local recruitment of operators and card punchers was intensive. In October 1951, the Agency's personnel office reported that it had placed recruiters in the U.S. Employment Service and in the Department of the Army Office of Employee Coordination, which allowed them to interview a steady flow of applicants.[59] They had contacts at the Civil Service Commission, and recruiters worked to acquire applicants from other government agencies, such as the Veterans Administration, Census

"I detested one thing about MPRO. The women had to do what we did and that was handle those boxes of cards and paper. I never liked that. The boxes were delivered to the area and were put in a corner. You had to pick them up, and it was heavy and hard lifting. Most of the time the fellows would help the girls."

Maurice Bush, 12 April 1999

Bureau, and Government Accounting Office, that announced reductions in force (RIFs). Usually hired as GG-2s, the lowest pay scale, operators and card punchers frequently requested transfers out of the machine division soon after they reported for duty. Considering the physical demands of the jobs, a significant level of dissatisfaction is not surprising:

– Tabulating machine operators will be required to stand for long periods and to lift and carry trays of cards weighing approximately 20 pounds.

– Keypunch machine operators will be required to sit at assigned machines for long periods.

– Both tabulating and keypunch machine operators, GS-5 and below, will be required to work rotating shifts in a noisy atmosphere due to the machines.

In most instances the skills and knowledge acquired in NSA-222 [IBM Branch] are not easily adapted to work in other branches, therefore time and money are expended unnecessarily when personnel request a transfer.[60]

Transfers were rare, and opportunities for advancement within the organization were limited, according to Maebelle Holmes, a college graduate who entered the Agency in 1949:

> I had just graduated from A&T and applied for a job. It seems that they were only accepting applications for key punch operator. I took the [typing] test, but didn't pass – not fast enough. But they notified me that I could get a job in the IBM section, wiring boards. I was in the 8th wing. There were more blacks than whites, but key punch was virtually all black except for the supervisors. They started me as a GG-2. I was promoted to GG-3, then GG-4 and when I got be a GG-5, I became a first line supervisor. I had about ten people working for me. I tried to get out. Openings would be posted on the board, and I would apply for something, but it was almost unknown to transfer. At that time, it seems like the whites would come in with no degree and in a little while they would move on up. They would go to lunch with the bosses, and would move right on up – not necessarily in the section in which they trained, but in another section across the aisle or in a different wing.
>
> I liked my job, but I felt that they weren't always fair to us.[61]

Novella Carr, who entered the Agency in January 1951, spent the first twenty years of her career in the machine processing (MPRO) organization. She talked not only about the lack of mobility, but also about the negative effect security had on the flow of information about job opportunities:

> I came to the Agency in January 1951 from the Veterans Administration where I was being riffed. I was in the 8th wing.

MPRO was divided into three wings. The 6th wing was the key punch operators and the 7th and 8th wings were tabulating equipment operators. When I went into the IBM [tabulating equipment] section it was 90 percent black, and the whites that were in there were not educated. All the supervisors were white. There were some black team captains and most of them had some college. And all the key punchers were black. Security was very tight. If you didn't have a need to know, you couldn't go into another section. We got to know some of the girls in key punch because the wings were open in the back and they would walk through our section to go to lunch. And you might know somebody in 213, which was all black, because you caught a ride with someone. So you never heard about vacancies. You didn't get transferred. You just stayed. Supervisors would change, and they would reorganize, but you just stayed.[62]

*   *   *   *

Few memories of Arlington Hall Station are more vivid than those of the stifling heat. In that time, before air conditioning, windows were left open and huge fans were used to circulate the hot, humid air. In climate, as well as culture, the Agency was a southern institution. That image is evoked with remarkable clarity by the words of Dorothy Amis, who began a thirty-four-year career in the Agency as a tabulating equipment operator.

> Arlington Hall was a beautiful place. You see it was a former school, and they had beautiful landscaped gardens in front of the headquarters building. If it got too hot in the evening, from 4 to 12, well, you could go out and sit on the benches in the park area. And if it didn't cool off, they would dismiss you for the evening. But in the morning, it would start getting hot around 10. We would work right by the window,

and all the windows were open. Novella was one of those people singing all of the time – singing and working on the machines. It was just a different environment.[63]

Front view of Arlington Hall Station headquarters building

Garden in rear of Arlington Hall Station headquarters building

It is the settled policy of the United States Government that there shall be no discrimination in Federal employment or in providing Federal services and facilities. – From the text of President Truman's message to Congress on civil rights, 3 February 1948, *New York Times.*

It is hereby declared to be the policy of the President that there shall be equality of treatment and opportunity for all persons in the armed services without regard to race, color, religion or national origin. – From Executive Order 9981, signed by Harry S. Truman, 26 July 1948.

Despite President Truman's call for fair employment in the federal government and the issuance of Executive Order 9981, the Russian plaintext traffic processing unit was essentially all black well into the 1950s, and African-Americans continued to predominate at the lower salary grades in the machine division. The standout exception to these realities was the hiring and placement of African-Americans by the Research and Development organization at AHS in 1948. During a period when the *New York Times* was accusing the Army of trying "to preserve a pattern of bigotry which caricatures the democratic cause in every corner of the world," [64] the Agency hired its first black engineer, Carroll Robinson. He was assigned to the development team charged with building the Agency's first in-house developed digital computer, ABNER 1. Mitchell Brown and Charles Matthews, graduates of Hilltop Radio-Electronics Institute, a black-owned electronics school open to African-Americans in Washington, D. C., were also hired in 1948. With the title of engi-

Carroll Robinson, the first African-American engineer at NSA (later photo)

Mitchell Brown

Charles Matthews (later photo)

neering technician, they too were placed in meaningful positions, working side by side with their white counterparts. By all accounts, the environment for African-Americans in the Research and Development organization was generally positive and conducive to professional growth. Carroll Robinson became the Agency's first African-American senior executive, retiring from federal service as an office chief. Mitchell Brown became an expert on technical devices and ended his career as test director of the Digital Voice Processor Consortium Test Program, which led to the selection of equipment for the secure telephone unit (STU) II. Charles Matthews was a project engineer on ABNER 1 (the first in-house designed digital computer), then SOLO, the Agency's first transistorized special-purpose computer. He went on to hold a succession of supervisory and middle-management positions before retiring in 1988. Interviewed in 1999, Mr. Matthews provided a glimpse of the African-American experience in the 1940s:

Hilltop Radio-Electronics Institute

> I was born in Washington and went to Dunbar High School. Toward the end of WWII, I went into the Army (Quartermaster Corps). I stayed in the Army about nine months, then when I returned I took advantage of the GI bill and took technical courses at Hilltop Radio-Electronics Institute. It was more or less a black counterpart to the Capital Radio Institute. The Agency was filled with graduates from Hilltop. I don't know how we found out about the Agency. To my knowledge the Agency didn't recruit, but I

"[After the war] I had to find a job. They didn't give electrical type work to blacks here, so I went on unemployment. As a veteran, I got 52-20. You got $20 for 52 months or $52 a month for 20 months, something like that. I would go to the VA every month to sign for my check, and eventually I met a guy there, Mr. Hollywood, and told him that I was looking for work and my classification was electrician. He said that he doubted that I could find any work as an electrician, but there was a guy who repaired radios who might accept an apprentice. This was a black engineer, Mr. Gresham, who worked at the Bureau of Standards on very classified stuff. He was very well qualified and he took me on. When I went back to VA for my 52-20 check and told Mr. Hollywood that I had a job as an apprentice, he said that if this man would open a school, he could send him all the personnel that he needs. This was the founding of Hilltop Radio, and I was the first student."

Mitchell Brown, 24 June 1999

and two others decided to apply. I was so anxious to get a job, I kept bugging them, and I was the first to get hired. That was in 1948. I was hired as an engineering technician, Grade 9 (subprofessional). It was a good start, but whites that were hired as engineering technicians with comparable experiences and sometimes less training were always hired at a higher grade than we were. Even though you were hired at a grade lower than your white counterpart, it was still a job, and it probably was a pretty good salary at the time – $2,100. Most of the blacks in the Agency at that time were making $1,440, and in the early '40s to mid- '40s most blacks in the government were in the custodial force or were messengers. Even with a college education, that was the extent of employment. Then they started hiring them as clerks. The best jobs for blacks at that time were with the post office.

Initially I started off tearing down equipment. Then the branch that I was in was tasked to work on the first digital computer, ABNER 1. We built ABNER 1. I wasn't the only black in the organization. Carroll Robinson was there. He was an engineer and was hired shortly after I was hired. W. C. Syphax, a black engineer was in there; he built the power supply factory. But the majority of the organization was white, and they reacted to us very well. I never had any negative experiences.

The Research and Development organization of the late 1940s to mid-1950s was not free of racism. In his interview, Mr. Brown supported the claim that white engineering technicians with less or comparable qualifications were hired at higher grades. Carroll Robinson noted that for many years blacks were not sent to overseas locations because of the commonly held belief that they would be unwelcome in the host country. These blots on the record notwithstanding, R & D in 1948 stands as a beacon of light in an otherwise dismal period in the Agency's history of black employment.[65]

A National Agency Check is a good indicator of a person's past life, but is of no assistance in determining that person's present security risk. The use of a polygraph for this purpose would reduce materially the security risk involved in granting interim clearances. . . . A recommendation to allow the use of this machine is now pending before the director. – AFSA-16 [Security Control Division] Monthly Operational Report, 12 January 1951

Authority for the purchase of two Keeler polygraph machines and the employment and training of five persons was granted by DirAFSA. – AFSA-16 Monthly Operational Summary, January 1951

Effort is being made to take advantage of a release of keypunch operators from the Bureau of the Census. Ninety keypunch applicants will be interviewed on 5 April 1951. – AFSA-02 Semi-Monthly Report for 16-31 March 1951

The confluence of increased hiring of African-Americans, primarily for low-wage jobs in machine processing and traffic processing, and the introduction of the polygraph as part of the security screening process resulted in a crack in the all-white Security Division of AFSA. Raymond Weir, Jr., a D.C. schoolteacher, had served in the Army in WWII under Captain Fred Hazard. In November 1951, now Major Hazard, a branch chief in the Security Division, recruited and hired Mr. Weir as a polygraph examiner – the black polygrapher for black applicants. He was a trailblazer, becoming the first African-American polygraph examiner in the United States, and arguably the first African-American in the profession anywhere in the world.

Raymond Weir, Jr., the first African-American polygraph examiner (later photo)

"Notwithstanding the current personnel strength position of the Agency, the conclusion has been reached in this Division that to handle the employment problems of the Vint Hill Farms operation, the interim operation at the new site and the certain turnover of personnel which is anticipated at the time of the main move to Fort Meade,[66] we must at this time hire three additional interrogation technicians. . . . The three individuals hired should be one female and two white male technicians. Experience indicates that the requirement for an additional colored technician does not exist."

Monthly Operational Summary, Security Division, March 1953; NSA/CSS Archives Accession No. 42468

Nevertheless, the Security Division – populated by individuals with investigative or law enforcement training, including FBI veteran S. Wesley Reynolds as the chief from May 1953 to December 1961 – was viewed by many as the most conservative Agency organization.[67] For years Ray Weir was restricted to interviewing only blacks at NSA. Not until the 1960s, and then only in careful stages, was he assigned a demographic cross-section of the Agency's applicants.

In December 1998, long after retiring as chief of the Investigations Division (M54), Mr. Weir recounted his story, including an amusing anecdote that illustrates the incongruity of locating an arm of the supersecret, intelligence agency in the heart of the black community:

I was directly recruited into a program I'd never heard of. I was a schoolteacher in Washington at the time and the guy who did the recruiting was Major Fred Hazard, who was in Security. They wanted a black polygraph examiner. They were processing a lot of women at the time, key punch operators, most of whom were black, and somebody decided that it might be good if they had a black person be a polygrapher. Their problem was there were no black polygraph examiners anywhere. The Agency hired me and sent me to school in Chicago.[68] I graduated in, I guess, December 1951.

When I came, there were no blacks in Security and there were none in Personnel.[69] Personnel and Security were collocated because we had to process their applicants. We were in the old Post Office building on "U" Street, and the Agency was trying to be very inconspicuous in the middle of a black neighborhood. They were trying to be inconspicuous, but they deposited the training school there, where all these white kids were coming. My boss, Fred Hazard, the guy that hired me, was a

former L.A. police officer, and he went around to a barber shop on U street to get his hair cut. He came back and said that when he went in the barber shop was full, but by the time he was finished, he and the barber were the only ones left. I told him that he must realize that the barber shop was the place where people met their neighbors for the day and heard the news, and he was in the way. Seriously, he looked like a cop, and so they made themselves scarce. Anyway, Security thought it was just wonderful that they were going to have a black person. But, of course, after I started to work for them, the problem was what did I do? Well, I was hired to test these black people who were being hired as key punch operators. I didn't mind; they were paying me the same salary, as if I were testing everybody. But there were days they weren't hiring [blacks] and I had nothing to do.

Well, I didn't think that would last. It finally came about that they had more people to interview than we had examiners, including me. I did work charts and that sort of thing to stay busy, but one day they said, 'Ray, do you think you could handle one of these white people?' I said, 'yes'. After the first one or two came in and I had no problem, it was understood that I could interview white men, preferably from the north. Then, that fell by the wayside a little bit later on, and I could interview white men from the south. [Eventually] there was nothing but young white girls to be interviewed, and my boss said, 'Ray, you think you can take one of these women?' and I said, 'yes'. I suppose this was in the 1960s, late '60s. This was the kind of thing that couldn't be rushed.

What the Agency wanted, what my supervisors wanted was to make sure that [whoever] I interviewed would not have a legitimate complaint about [the interview]. I don't think that most of what I ran into in the Agency was prejudice, per se. There was an unwillingness to do things which would create problems, an unwillingness to do things which would cause any kind of publicity.

Ray Weir rose to the top of his profession, becoming the first African-American president of the American Polygraph Association and a recognized industry expert who testified before the United States Senate Ethics Committee in its 1979 financial misconduct investigation of Senator Herman Talmadge (D-Ga).[70]

During the 1940s the Office of Operations probably consistently followed the military model, i.e., all black functional units were normally formed within larger white organizations. Herman Phynes, for example, was head of the commercial code section, which is believed to have remained a segregated unit until it folded (probably around 1950). Bill Coffee, after leaving that section, supervised a group of typists that transcribed automatic Morse tapes. It is doubtful that this was a mixed group. An indication of the personal feelings and controversy that might have surrounded these black units is provided by a story told by Jack Gurin, chief of the Russian plaintext exploitation branch in 1948. According to Jack, the critical need for clerical support prompted him to approach the personnel officer with a request for additional typists. He was told that "Code 1's" were not available, but "Code 2's" could be obtained. The coding, it was explained, was used on personnel records to designate race. "Code 1" was white; "Code 2" was "colored." On the advice of the personnel officer, Gurin discussed with the existing branch personnel the possibility of bringing "Negroes" into the unit. One person, "a very dignified, good-looking Alabama lady, objected, stating that she could not 'sit next to a colored person and work'." Gurin relocated her desk, and shortly thereafter an African-American man and five women reported for duty.[71] Once again, however, this was an all-black functional unit, in this case a typing section, within a larger white organization.

Signs of change began to appear around 1950. According to Dave Bryant, by that year he had secured a transfer out of AFSA-213, the traffic processing branch, and was attending Russian language classes preparatory to working as a translator/analyst in the Russian plaintext branch. James Pryde was another early escapee from "the plantation." A former radio operator with the Tuskegee airmen, he joined the Agency in 1950 and was initially assigned to AFSA-213 and then the mailroom. Eventually, however, it was discovered that he could read automatic Morse tapes, and he was transferred to a signals analysis section. A brilliant career in Soviet exploitation followed, first as an analyst, then as a manager and as a senior executive.[72]

James Pryde
(later photo)

An equally significant development in the early 1950s was the hiring of African-Americans as entry-level analysts and linguists and, for the first time, their immediate integration into a target element, bypassing the traffic processing division altogether. Both Clarence Toomer and Arthur Davis graduated from Howard University in 1950, Mr. Toomer as a premed major, Mr. Davis with a concentration in German. In 1951, Mr. Toomer was an accounting clerk at the Census Bureau. Seeking a better position, he registered with the Labor Department as a job applicant and was subsequently interviewed at the Pentagon by a representative of the Department of Defense, in reality someone from AFSA. He was hired and entered on duty as a GS-4 cryptanalytic aide. Art Davis, meanwhile, had responded to an advertisement in the local newspaper for government linguists. He too joined the Agency in 1951 and was placed in an intensive Russian language course. There he met his future sister-in-law, Royolla Franklin Davis, a newly hired GS-5 Slavic languages major from the University of California at Berkeley. Following their initial training, Clarence Toomer, Art Davis, and Royolla Franklin Davis worked as junior professionals in major Soviet exploitation divisions.[73]

Minnie McNeal, a native of Philadelphia, worked at the Commerce Department in Philadelphia, then the Census Bureau in Washington, after graduating from the Philadelphia High School for Girls. She also never worked in the all-black traffic division or in machine processing, but in a 1999 interview, she described how she narrowly escaped that fate:

Minnie McNeal Kenny
(later photo)

I came to be interviewed at Arlington Hall in 1951, and there was a woman. I don't know her name, but she was white and she had also graduated from the Philadelphia High School for Girls. She recognized my class ring, and she not only hired me, she vowed that I would not be 'going down in the hole'. I didn't have the slightest idea what she was talking about. I was just glad that I had a job. I went for processing, and when I came back, she assigned me upstairs. There was a group of us [including] Barbara Barnes, Bess [nfi], and Priscilla [nfi] [upstairs]. Most of the blacks at that time were assigned to the basement. We were [in] the first group whose initial assignment was upstairs in Operations in B Building. We were assigned to the 'U' Street School, and we stayed there until we got our clearances or whatever. We came as a group to the organization. We all worked under Sam Hall on what they call ALLO [all other targets]. We were dispersed throughout the place.[74]

Clarence Toomer, Art Davis, Royolla Franklin Davis, and Minnie McNeal Kenny represented a new breed of African-American employee in the Operations Directorate. They were hired at the GS-4 or GS-5 level, higher than the starting grades offered to African-Americans in MPRO or Russian plaintext traffic processing and equivalent to that given most whites with comparable qualifications. They were immediately placed in intensive training programs to prepare them for professional careers as a linguist or cryptanalyst, and upon completion of training, they were assigned to substantive target exploitation problems in a totally integrated environment. Not until well after they entered on duty did they learn of the existence of AFSA-213. Fellow Howard University graduates who were also hired by the Agency, but sent to "the snakepit," asked Clarence Toomer how it happened that he was assigned to an analytic organization. He did not have an answer.

How were these young professional people of color received in the workplace? The reports are mixed. Most said that the work environment was, at least superficially, generally free of racial overtones. Their desks were intermixed with the others; they occasionally ate lunch with their white colleagues in the cafeteria; and advanced training in the core disciplines of the agency – language, traffic analysis, and cryptanalysis – was readily obtained. But they still experienced the occasional slight; racial slurs were overheard in office conversation; and few African-Americans were assigned to the organization working on the highest priority Russian systems. Tours at external locations were difficult to come by, and as their careers progressed, there appeared to be a "glass ceiling" that dictated, at the executive level, that they were usually the "bridesmaid," or deputy, seldom the bride.

The sense of an undercurrent of racial bias was understandable. In the early fifties, not only were the all-black enclaves still very much in operation inside the Agency, but the external environment was still essentially segregated. Eugene Becker, who retired as the assistant deputy director for support services in 1992, described aspects of Washington life and the Armed Forces Security Agency when he entered on duty in January 1952.

> I was struck by the fact that the bus that I rode out to Arlington Hall was a segregated bus, because you transferred from the District bus and trolley to Virginia buses at the Federal Triangle. So I got on the bus that took you to Arlington, and it was segregated. This was 1952. I remember being struck by that. Having gone to school in the district [George Washington University], I knew that the movie theaters were segregated. I remember going to the Blue Mirror. That was the club where you had whites and Afro-Americans mixing. There were not many of them. But I had never given it a thought that the bus system in Northern Virginia was still segregated. Washington in those days was a Southern town, totally dominated by Southern culture.

> The fellow that I talked to in my interview was clearly on the Russian problem. I could decipher that much from his questions and the way he inquired about my interests, but before my final clearance came through, it was decided that I would go in a class. I think there were five of us that started in an Arabic class. I think that it was the first one begun at the Agency.

> We went to the school on U Street and 14th, the old post office building, for six months. We had a great instructor. The agency language department was excellent at that time. We were in an all-white class, as were most of the classes. I don't remember seeing any Afro-Americans in the language classes at the time. There may have been one or two that came in while we were going through our six-month period, but on reporting for work in January, I don't remember seeing any in the school.

> The Agency is a microcosm of the nation at large. It was neither ahead of it or behind it, and so it reflected, to a precise degree, what was going on – what the country was. The workforce had a liberal cast, but seeded among the workforce were plenty of racists. They were not hard to find. That was palpable in the place. You knew who they were.[75]

> "[In Washington], we went to our own segregated areas. We went to our own clubs, our own theaters. We had nice theaters, nice clubs, so you didn't realize you were being segregated that much. It wasn't something that was bothersome. We had the Lincoln theater, the Booker T., and in northeast [Washington], we had the Strand theater."
>
> Carroll Robinson, 8 June 1999

*   *   *   *

By the mid-fifties, there were even positive changes within the traffic processing division (now designated NSA-63) and the machine section. Carl Dodd, an NSA-63 supervisor, drafted job descriptions for the other leaders in the organization which eventually were approved and resulted in an upgrade of all positions in the division.[76] An interview with William Pinchback, however, revealed that although measured progress had been achieved by 1955, remnants of the old practices were still very much evident. Mr. Pinchback, a former Army cryptologic operator and a 1950 graduate of Storer College, entered on duty in 1954 as a GS-3 communications clerk in NSA-63. He was assigned to a recently added branch that received, sorted, and distributed hard copy messages (other than Russian plaintext radioprinter). At that time, he recalled, whites were occasionally hired and assigned to his unit and that one, with only a high school diploma, was brought in at a higher grade than he. The system was slowly changing, however, for this time, after the unfairness was brought to the attention of the section chief, Mr. Pinchback was promoted with less than the minimum time in grade. The next year, Mr. Pinchback applied for an advertised vacancy for a cryptanalytic aide. In a then rare demonstration of equal opportunity in competitive selection, he was interviewed and chosen for the job. Once in his new office, his supervisor confided that Pinchback's army experience as a code clerk, coupled with the scores that he achieved on Agency aptitude tests, indicated that he would be a good cryptanalyst. In the mid-fifties, though, these facts and a college degree had not prevented a black man from being hired as a GS-3 and being initially assigned to the mailroom in the National Security Agency.[77]

Significant professional advancement for African-Americans in the machine division during the 1950s was limited, but James Bostic broke convention. In 1952 he left the Census Bureau and joined AFSA as a tabulating equipment operator. A gifted, largely self-taught programmer and systems analyst, he became known as the "the Optimizer" during a career that paralleled the agency's advancements in computer technology. An early tour in ABNER 1 operations was followed by assignment as a programmer on ABNER 2 and as a software designer for a mass file storage and retrieval system. Before retiring in 1986, he led the terminal subsystem development team for a UNIX-based system.[78]

James Bostic, "The Optimizer" (undated from the 1970s)

* * * *

The Research and Development organization, already home to a number of African-American males in engineering specialties, was also breaking other barriers in 1951. Vera Shoffner Russell, an African-American mathematician, reported to the Agency that year and was assigned as a programmer on the early computers, ABNER 2, ATLAS 1, and ATLAS 2. But the glass was only half full. She believes, as do the vast majority of African-Americans hired before 1954, that she started at a lower grade than similarly qualified whites. Her story also includes familiar references to the employment options for educated blacks in the 1950s and to the harsh realities of segregation:

I graduated in 1951 from West Virginia State College and took the test for math majors at the U.S. Employment Center in Charleston. I was a math and physics

major and had an offer to teach school in Winston-Salem [North Carolina], but I didn't want to teach. At the time, however, for the most part, when [blacks] came out of college, you went to teach. Teaching and preaching were the only things open. Then, I got this letter to come to Washington and take a physical at the Pentagon. Shortly thereafter, I came into the Agency, which was located at the time on Arlington Boulevard. Now, my maiden name was Shoffner, and West Virginia is only three percent black, so my notification of hiring, which I saw in my personnel folder years later, carried a 'w', and they offered me a GS-5. When I got here, they asked if I would accept a 4. I took it. I didn't know anything about

GS ratings, and I really think they offered me the job because they thought I was white. As far as segregation goes, I did better in West Virginia, because Washington would make you stand in carry-out lines. But you didn't have that in West Virginia. The first year I came here, I sat up at the drugstore counter down on Connecticut Avenue, and I opened the compartment and took a donut. And all the commotion! All the waitresses were white, and they kept going back and forth – passing me. I wanted a cup of coffee, and nobody gave me a cup. So, the guy from behind the cigar counter came up and told me, 'We do not serve colored people at the counter'.[79]

Vera Russell
(later photo)

Epilogue

> I was so involved in what the Agency stood for, and I wanted it to be better. I had a feeling that things were going to get better. Everybody in there was not evil. I felt that one day African-Americans would break out of this box and be able to go into reporting or personnel or other areas, if they were prepared. I preached – be prepared. – Iris Carr, 30 June 1999

In 1956, as part of a major Agency reorganization, NSA-63, the successor to AFSA-213 and AFSA-211 (another receipt and distribution unit with a high percentage of African-Americans), was dissolved. Many blacks, particularly the tape printers, moved to the new collection organization where they continued to perform the tasks of receiving, converting, and distributing intercept data. A large number of the scanners, however, and many who had worked on the staff of NSA-63 were transferred to various divisions in GENS, Office of General Studies, where they successfully pursued careers as analysts, staff officers, and managers.

As a group, African-Americans suffered from institutional racism at Arlington Hall Station. The segregationist policies of the Army were strictly enforced during the war years and, with the singular exception of Research and Development, were generally followed for years thereafter. It was a white-male-dominated environment that reflected Army racial policies and southern attitudes. African-Americans were routinely hired at lower grades and shuffled into the most menial jobs. They waited longer for fewer promotions and received less training, which constrained their opportunities to assume higher-paying positions.

Early in the 1950s, as the Army's long-standing support for the "separate, but equal" doctrine faded, barriers at AHS began to crumble. African-Americans were hired not only as keypunchers and clerks, but also as analytic aides, linguists, and mathematicians. Some that had entered the Agency through the all-black traffic processing division successfully transferred to organizations that held the promise for challenging, rewarding work in a racially integrated environment. The contributions of whites who acted as agents for change during this period cannot be overlooked or underestimated. African-Americans who started their careers during the early fifties and rose to leadership positions acknowledged the assistance and mentorship of many Caucasians, several of whom, Melba McCarthy, Benson Buffham, and Jack Gurin, were interviewed for this manuscript.

The dissolution of NSA-63 erased a visible and notorious manifestation of racial separation, but questions about equality in recruitment, hiring, assignments, job training, awards, and promotions continued to be raised for years afterwards. Many of those who started at Arlington Hall Station became the Agency's social activists of the 1960s and 1970s at its new location, Fort Meade, Maryland. There, new chapters in the African-American experience at NSA would be written.

End Notes

1. Alan M. Osur, *Blacks in the Army Air Forces during WWII: The Problem of Race Relations* (Washington, D.C., 1977), 11.

2. Bernard C. Nalty and Morris J. MacGregor, eds., *Blacks in the Military: Essential Documents* (Wilmington, DE, 1981), 108.

3. Ulysses Lee, *The Employment of Negro Troops* (Washington, D.C., 1994), 111-112.

4. Nalty and MacGregor, *Blacks in the Military*, 114-115.

5. Osur, *Blacks in the Army Air Forces during WWII*, 5.

6. Lee, *The Employment of Negro Troops*, 45.

7. Osur, *Blacks in the Army Air Forces during WWII*, 5.

8. Charles H. Wesley, *The Quest for Equality: From the Civil War to Civil Rights* (Cornwell Heights, PA, 1969), 176.

9. CCH oral history interview with Carl Dodd, 14 July 1999.

10. NSA predecessor organizations carried various names between 1930 and 1952, i.e., Signal Intelligence Section, Signals Security Service, Signal Security Branch, Signal Security Division, Signal Security Agency, Army Security Agency, and Armed Forces Security Agency.

11. Frank B. Rowlett, *The Story of Magic: Memoirs of an American Cryptologic Pioneer* (Laguna Hills, CA, 1998), 47.

12. James L. Gilbert and John P. Finnegan, eds., *U.S. Army Signals Intelligence in World War II*, (Washington, D.C.: Center of Military History, 1993), 26-27.

13. *History of the Signal Security Agency*, Vol. 1, Part 1, Organization, 12-16, 38-52.

14. Personnel records of Bernard W. Pryor and interview with Delores Schommer, 6 May 1999, who entered on duty with SIS on 16 July 1940. According to Mrs. Schommer, Bernie was the single messenger for the organization.

15. Constance McLaughlin Green, *The Secret City: A History of Race Relations in the Nation's Capital* (Princeton, NJ, 1967), 231. According to records maintained by the Office of Workforce Information, Official of Personnel Management, the total number of civilians employed by the federal government in 1938 was 882,226.

16. Personnel Clearances and Historical Study, NSA Archives-ACC#17862.

17. Memo from E.S. Turner, Adjutant General, to Chief Signal Officer, 18 April 1942, NSA Archives – ACC#18981.

18. *History of the Signal Security Agency*, Vol. 1, Part 1, 88.

19. NARA RG457, Box 1027, Signal Security Agency – Personal Interviews, July 15-September 1943.

20. CCH oral history interview, General Earle F. Cooke, 15 July 1982.

21. Personnel Records, William D. Coffee.

22. Tom Standage, *The Victorian Internet* (New York, 1998), 112-116.

23. *History of the Signal Security Agency*, Volume Two: The General Cryptanalytic Problem, 229-230.

24. Ibid.

25. Memo for the Control Officer, SSA, from SPSIS-9 (Intelligence Branch), 15 September 1944, RG457, Box 1005, ACC#10616.

26. Mission and functions, B-3-b and organizational charts, 15 November 1944 and 1 February 1945, NARA, RG457, Box 843, ACC#646.

27. Ibid.

28. Mission and functions, B-3-b; CCH oral history interview with Benson K. Buffham, 15 June 1999.

29. Mission and functions, B-3-b; personnel records of Herman Phynes.

30. Personnel records of Bernard Pryor.

31. The plans and priorities officer developed collection plans and adjusted the tasking for intercept sites to meet changing requirements.

32. CCH oral history interview with Benson K. Buffham, 15 June 1999.

33. B-3-b organizational chart, NARA RG457, Box 843, ACC#646.

34. Intercept and Control Branch Annual Report, 1945-1946; NSA/CSS Archives, ACC#17394; personnel records, William D. Coffee.

35. Annual Report of the Cryptanalytic Branch, July 1945-June 1946; NSA/CSS Archives ACC#47439 and personnel records of Herman Phynes.

36. *History of the Signal Security Agency,* Volume 11: The Machine Branch, published by ASA, Washington, D.C., 1948.

37. CCH oral history interview with Norm Willis, 11 January 1999.

38. Dr. Solomon Kullback was one of the three pioneering "junior cryptanalysts" hired by William Friedman in April 1930. Harry Lawrence Clark joined SIS later that year as a cryptographic clerk to analyze secret inks. Sam Snyder entered on duty with SIS in 1936 and worked as a cryptanalyst on both Italian and Japanese systems prior to WWII. Colonel Spencer Ball Akin was O.I.C., Signal Intelligence Service, 25 July 1939-2 May 1941.

39. CCH oral history interview with Delores Schommer, 5 May 1999.

40. Phone interview with David Shepard, 22 May 2000.

41. CCH oral history interview with Geneva Trusty Arthur, 28 September 1999.

42. History of GENS-6 Civil Division of Office of General Studies; NSA/CSS Archives, ACC#9895, and CCH oral history interviews with Jacob Gurin on 26 April 1995 and 15 October 1999.

43. CCH oral history interviews with Jacob Gurin, 26 April 1995 and 15 October 1999, and David Bryant, 23 February 1999.

44. Thomas R. Johnson, *American Cryptology during the Cold War, 1945-1989, Book I: The Struggle for Centralization, 1945-1960* (CCH-E32-95-03), 168.

45. 27 March 1950 memorandum from C.P. Collins, Chairman USCIB Intelligence Committee to Coordinator of Joint Operations; NSA/CSS Archives, ACC#8243.

46. Report by the Director, Armed Forces Security Agency, to the Armed Forces Security Council on Requirements for Conduct of an Optimum Communication Intelligence Program, 14 July 1950; NSA/CSS Archives, ACC#5221.

47. From 1949 until sometime in 1951, AFSA-213 was a branch. A December 1951 organizational chart shows AFSA-213 as a division. A reorganization in August 1952 resulted in a new designator, AFSA-29. When NSA was created, AFSA-29 became NSA-63. In the interest of simplicity and consistency, the Russian radioprinter traffic processing division will usually be referred to by the earlier designator, AFSA-213.

48. Undated and unsigned report; however, a penciled notation indicates it was authored before 31 May 1950; NSA/CSS Archives ACC#8243. Data extracts from the paper later appeared in the 14 July 1950 report from the director, AFSA, to the Armed Forces Security Council.

49. NSA oral history interview with William Jones conducted by R.D. Farley on 14 August 1986.

50. CCH oral history interview with Richard Hill, 18 October 1999. The low grade structure was confirmed in other interviews and by the personnel records of Jefferson Tancil, a supervisor in the traffic division. From January 1950 to November 1951, he was a GS-6 section chief responsible for eighteen to thirty communications clerks, GG-2 to GG5.

51. CCH oral history interviews: William Byrd on 8 March 1999; Richard Hill on 18 October 1999; and Carl Dodd (by phone), 17 May 1999.

52. CCH oral history interview with Bernice Mills on 10 November 1999.

53. Jack Gurin interview, 15 October 1999.

54. Comptroller Monthly Operational Summary, July 1953; NSA/CSS Archives, ACC#42468.

55. CCH oral history interview with Iris Carr, 16 June 1999.

56. Report by the Director, AFSA, to the Armed Forces Security Agency Council, 14 July 1950, 3; NSA/CSS Archives, ACC#5221.

57. Ibid., 36.

58. AFSA-02 Semi-Monthly Report for 16-31 March 1951; NSA/CSS Archives ACC#42468.

59. AFSA-153 Monthly Operational Summary, October 1951; NSA/CSS; NSA/CSS Archives, ACC#42468.

60. Memorandum, "Excessive Number of Transfer Requests," from Deputy Head, NSA-222 (IBM Branch) to NSA-220A (Assistant Chief for Administrative Management, Machine Division), 2 December 1952; NSA/CSS Archives ACC#2606.

61. Oral history interview with Maebelle Holmes, 26 April 1999.

62. Oral history interview with Novella Carr, 19 January 1999.

63. CCH oral history interview with Dorothy Amis, 19 February 1999.

64. Morris J. MacGregor, Jr., *Integration of the Armed Forces*, 1940-1965, (Washington,D.C.: Center for Military History, 1989), 363, footnote 81.

65. Information in this chapter obtained from the following oral history interviews: Carroll Robinson, 8 June 1999; Charles Matthews, 22 June 1999; Mitchell Brown, 24 June 1999.

66. By 1949 AFSA had outgrown the temporary buildings and converted dormitories at Arlington Hall Station. Also, in the wake of the national angst over the Soviet Union's first nuclear test, AFSA was directed by the JCS to identify a standby or disaster site outside the metropolitan Washington area. The two requirements were merged, and Fort Knox, Kentucky, was selected as the site for a new headquarters and operations building. This decision was reversed, however, when the prospect of massive civilian resignations became apparent, and the search continued. Several sites in northern Virginia and Maryland were considered, but on 5 February 1952 Fort Meade was officially chosen as the new location for AFSA.

67. Other examples of appointments to the Office of Security: Two former FBI employees and one former ONI employee were chosen to become the Special Research Unit (investigations of alleged employee wrongdoings). Monthly Operational Summaries, Security Division, February and March 1953; NSA/CSS ACC#42468.

68. Chicago was the home of the Keeler Institute, the training school for polygraph examiners.

69. This is inaccurate. At least one African-American, Bernie Pryor, was an employee counselor in the personnel division at this time.

70. *Polygraph: Journal of the American Polygraph Association*, December 1979, Vol. 8, No. 4.

71. CCH interview with Jack Gurin, 15 October 1999.

72. CCH interview with James Pryde, 15 December 1998.

73. CCH oral history interviews with Clarence Toomer, 12 January 2000, and Arthur Davis, 8 February 2000.

74. CCH oral history interviews with Minnie McNeal Kenny, 30 March 1999. ALLO targets were those other than the Soviet Union.

75. CCH oral history interview with Eugene Becker, 19 January 1999.

76. CCH oral history interview with Carl Dodd, 2 April 1999.

77. CCH oral history interview with William Pinchback, 25 January 1999.

78. CCH oral history interview with James Bostic, 4 November 1999.

79. CCH oral history interview with Vera Russell, 8 February 1999.

*J*eannette Williams retired from the National Security Agency in 1998 after thirty-five years of service. During the 1960s and 1970s, at the height of the arms race, she was an intelligence analyst and reported extensively on missile and space activities. Later in her career, she assumed successively responsible management positions, including assignments as the Agency's senior operational officer and as an assistant inspector general. Since retiring from federal service, Mrs. Williams has been employed as a principal research analyst with Logicon DPC Technologies under contract to NSA.

Mrs. Williams holds a degree in English from Ohio State University and is a graduate of the Federal Executive Institute and the National Senior Cryptologic Course. She resides in Carroll County, Maryland, with her husband, Walter, and enjoys the arts, gardening, reading, and community affairs.

*M*s. Dickerson began her career at NSA in 1967 in computer operations. After holding numerous analytic and administrative positions, Ms. Dickerson worked in the National Cryptologic School as an education and training officer and adjunct faculty member. While at the School, she served as a member of a career development panel. A member of Women in NSA, Ms. Dickerson assisted in education and career advancement for women in the Agency. Toward the end of her career, she served in the Center for Cryptologic History as a historian. After retiring from NSA in 1998, Ms. Dickerson worked under contract as a senior systems analyst in the NSA Technology Support Division and later as a senior research analyst in the Center for Cryptologic History.

A graduate of the University of Baltimore, Ms. Dickerson holds a B.A. degree in sociology and business management. She is married, the parent of four and grandmother of four. Ms. Dickerson resides in Anne Arundel County, Maryland, and presently works at the Museum of Industry in Baltimore, Maryland, as a docent coordinator.